STEPHEN GABRIEL

Hope
for Your Grandchildren

Talking to the Third Generation about What Matters

Scepter

Published by Scepter Publishers, Inc.
info@scepterpublishers.org
www.scepterpublishers.org
800-322-8773
New York

Text design: PerfecType, Nashville, TN
Cover Design: Studio Red Design, Washington, DC
Cover Image: Shutterstock.com

Library of Congress Control Number: 2021947550
ISBN Paperback: 9781594174445
ISBN eBook: 9781594174452

Printed in the United States of America

To the memory of my grandson, John Paul Kilner,
whose short life touched so many.

Contents

Introduction

If you were to speak to your grandchildren and great-grandchildren about the important issues for a person of faith, what would you tell them? What message do you want them to understand, so that they, in turn, will take it seriously and pass it on to their progeny?

The topics that follow are designed to be a guide that will help you to formulate your own personal discussions with your young adult grandchildren. Each chapter includes personal notes to my grandchildren from the depths of my soul. It is hoped that these notes will serve as examples or templates to encourage you to generate ideas for your personal letters or discussions.

You need to make it your own, with your personal stories that your grandchildren will remember for the rest of their lives. You will have a greater impact on your grandchildren's faith than you realize. I pray that this book will serve you well.

Each part is intentionally short, intended to give you a few ideas that will generate others. The goal is to introduce or reinforce some important ideas and encourage young people to think about them, and with hope, to take them seriously.

One | God

My Dear Grandchildren,

Do you believe in God? I do! I have always believed in God, even when I was a college student and somewhat of a lost soul. I was truly a prodigal son for several years. No, I didn't get into drugs, disown my family, or spend all my inheritance on booze. But I was wandering in a "distant land" throughout my college years until the beginning of graduate school. As I'm sure you will experience, or have already experienced, the college campus is truly another planet—an alternate universe that makes it easy to believe God doesn't exist or, at least, that God doesn't care about having any kind of relationship with you. I fell into this life too. It was easier this way. I didn't try to enter a relationship with God. Frankly, I didn't know how! I thought, why should I get out of bed in the morning to worship someone I don't know and who doesn't know me, for all I knew? The truth is, I made little, if any, effort to learn about God and how he expresses his love for me. I had enough studying to do! Looking back, I see what a risky time this was for me, for many reasons, but especially because I could have easily fallen in love with the wrong person. I could have easily married someone who lived her life like me, but didn't hold the values I truly held dear. Someone with no faith. I believe this would have made my path toward embracing my faith in God a lot more difficult. But by God's grace I fell in love with your grandmother instead.

It's a funny, but actually quite frightening, reality that you can live your life as if you believe in one thing (or in nothing), but all along—at your core—you truly believe in something quite different. And then, some moment in your life strips that charade bare and you realize the way you have been living your life doesn't actually reflect who you really are at all. The prospect of marriage and children was that moment for me. Becoming a husband and realizing I would be a father moved me to take life more seriously and examine how I lived my life.

I was raised Catholic, but my parents didn't have the tools to really give me the formation I needed to be anything more than a "Mass on Sunday because that's just what we do" kind of Catholic. They did what most good parents did. They made sure I attended the parish religious education program when I wasn't attending a Catholic school. I can see now that that wasn't enough. Still, because that's what I knew, I started there. It wasn't just a question of how I wanted to live my life now, it was a question of how I hoped my children would live their lives. And like all fathers, I wanted more for my children than I ever wanted for myself. I wanted them to be happy and fulfilled, and I knew ignoring God wasn't giving me that. When you have children, you will see what I mean.

For some people, returning to God and finally recognizing his immense love for you is a somewhat magical moment, perhaps something difficult to explain. It's a moment of submission, humility, and maybe even a leap of faith. For me, however, it was a slow awakening as I dove deeper and deeper into the teaching of the Catholic Church. But, honestly, the more I saw how easy reason makes it to believe in God, the more I became convinced that faith in God is not just a leap of faith—it's logic, too. In fact, it seemed to take much more work to argue the opposite. This was how I began to open my heart up to God and ask him to return to my life. Not as romantic as a flash of light or a miraculous sign. But God knew me and how my brain worked.

I cannot prove that God exists in the sense that I have seen him and spoken with him face-to-face. God, of course, is a spiritual being. He is not a physical being. He has no body, no arms and legs. We all have a difficult time wrapping our heads around that fact. Many scientists, certainly not all, have so much trouble with this fact that they deny his existence because they can't prove his existence based on the material world in which they operate. Scientists simply don't have all the tools needed to address whether God exists or not.

Reading the works of philosophers, such as Peter Kreeft, further opened my eyes to the truth that faith doesn't defy reason. For example, we can use philosophical reasoning and the simple observance of the world in which we live to conclude that God does indeed exist and that he created the universe and all that is in it. You might start by considering the order and design that we can observe in the world.

If you arrived at a deserted island and found seashells arranged on the beach in words that said, "Please help me. I'm starving," would you assume that the waves washed up those shells over a period of time in such a way that these words were formed? The likelihood that that could have happened is infinitesimal, indeed. Of course, you would have immediately concluded that someone arranged those shells to send a message to whoever might see it. The message was not the result of random events. Rather, there was someone with the intelligence to form those words and convey its message.

There are many other proofs or ways that convinced me that it makes sense that God exists. I frequently consider my purpose in life. Anything without a purpose is expendable. It can be disposed of. Activities without purpose are a waste of time. If God does not exist and I am the product of a random process, then my life has no purpose. Indeed, nothing has any ultimate purpose. In such a world, morality is devoid of meaning. Being kind and doing the "right thing" are purely acts of utility. For an intelligent being, such a world is truly depressing. I prefer to live in a world with purpose and meaning, a world created by God. Am I just fooling myself so I feel better about life? I don't think so. We all have this desire for purpose and meaning that was put there by our Creator. The world makes more sense if it has purpose, if it has a creator who instilled us with a purpose.

So, I cannot see God like I can see material beings. However, I can see the results of his work, his creation. I can see a world exquisitely designed, I experience love and my own consciousness. I see beauty and experience virtue. I see people employ their freedom to do good and evil. I experience remorse and repentance. Are these just a series of biochemical reactions in the brain caused by chance? I don't think so!

I hope my experience will be helpful to you. You may have doubts about the existence of God because he doesn't present himself to us the way people do, the way creation does. However, I urge you to reflect on God's existence carefully, and make the effort to find the answers to your questions. If you do, you will be blessed with a life rich with meaning.

Affectionately,
Grandpa

Two | The Gospels

My Dear Grandchildren,

I worry when I hear people refer to the Gospels as "myths" or nice stories with moral messages. Scholars have been studying the Gospels and the basis for their acceptance for centuries. But most people don't go to the trouble to verify the credibility of the Gospels on their own. We rely on people we trust, such as our parents, our theology or religion teachers, and others. However, when we hear from others, such as university professors, that the Gospels are merely myths, our faith can be shaken.

What basis do we have for believing that the Gospels are anything other than myths popularized by overzealous followers of a charismatic preacher? Is there reason to believe that the Gospels are credible?

I don't believe the Gospels are just myths. Rather, I believe they are reliable accounts of the teaching and events in the life of Jesus. Here's why.

First of all, there is significant historical and archeological evidence. For example, the pagan historian Tacitus, in his *Annals*, which was written around AD 120, referred to Christ as the founder of the Christian religion and the fact that he was crucified by Pontius Pilate.[1] He was writing about how Nero, the Roman emperor, blamed the AD 64 fire in Rome on the Christians. Pliny the Younger, in his *Letters* (AD 112), also wrote about the Christians and how they worshiped Christ as a god. These pagan works were written some eighty to ninety years after the death of Christ.[2]

1. Tacitus, *Annals*, 15:44.
2. Pliny the Younger, *Letters*, Book 10, Letter 96.

There have also been numerous archeological discoveries of coins and other artifacts that bear the names of people and places identified in the Gospels, such as Nazareth, Herod Agrippa, Pontius Pilate, and Caiaphas. These discoveries validate many of the details found in the Gospels.

A number of ancient copies exist of full or partial Greek New Testament manuscripts. For example, Papyrus 52 contains the Gospel passage John 18, which details Jesus' betrayal, arrest, and judgment and is dated around AD 100–150.

So, we can establish that Jesus lived. But did he really say the things and do the things reported in the Gospels? Most importantly, did he, in fact, rise from the dead? Is it possible that these miraculous happenings were simply made up by his followers?

Being reasonable people, we don't fall for every wild story told to us by anyone who happens to come along. We expect proof or at least some reasonable basis for believing the stories that are told to us. Many people discount the veracity of the Gospels simply because of the miraculous events that are reported in them. Certainly, miracles are not normal. We don't get up in the morning and expect to witness the miraculous sometime during the course of the day. But is it reasonable to believe that miracles are possible? Well, if we believe that an intelligent being created the world and everything in it by the force of his will, then it's reasonable to believe that he can perform the occasional miracle when it suits him. Right? No doubt, any sane, well-grounded person will approach claims of miraculous events with a degree of skepticism. However, a reasonable person should be prepared to accept that a miracle occurred if adequate evidence is provided or based on the testimony of trustworthy witnesses.

The dating of the Gospels is important in this regard. Few scholars date any of the Gospels after AD 100. Few, if any scholars, date the Gospel of Mark much after AD 70, and many scholars date the synoptic Gospels (Matthew, Mark, and Luke) in the AD 60s. Hence, the Gospels were written within thirty to sixty years after the death of Jesus. The oral tradition of the life of Christ was well established by this time. Errors in these written accounts would have been challenged strenuously. Indeed, there were likely some of Jesus' followers still alive who would have challenged any mistakes in these written accounts.

Not having spent much time reading the Gospels in my teens and most of my twenties, other than listening to readings at Mass, I had not thought much about their importance or whether or not I should believe them. However, in my thirties, I committed myself to really growing closer to God and began reading the Gospels every day for a few minutes. I can tell you now that knowledge of the Gospels is essential to gaining greater knowledge of God. As St. Jerome said, "Ignorance of the Scripture is ignorance of Christ." Now I try to read the Gospels prayerfully. I reflect on what I've read in the day's Gospel reading and take it to my prayer. I have found this to be crucial for fostering a friendship with Jesus.

Finally, we have to ask ourselves, what motive would the early Christians have had for fabricating the miracles and, most importantly, the resurrection of Christ from the dead?

The evidence points to the existence of Christ and the fact that many Christians lived and were persecuted in Rome in AD 64, just thirty years after the death of Christ. It is likely that among those people were some who either knew Jesus, knew of Jesus, or were close to someone who knew or knew of him. They certainly didn't suffer their persecutions for a faith they knew to be false.

In the first three hundred years or so of Christianity, the Christian's lot was not one of status, wealth, and privilege. Rather, Christians faced persecution and, frequently, a horrible death. If Jesus was merely a charismatic preacher who put himself on a pedestal—saying that he was the Son of God the Father; that he was "the way, the truth and the life"; that his followers should eat his flesh and drink his blood; and many other seemingly outrageous things—and then was viciously crucified by the Romans at the request of the Jewish authorities, why would his followers make up stories about miracles and his resurrection from the dead?

What was in it for them? Embracing their Christian beliefs led to their persecution by the Jews and the Romans. Most of Jesus' followers would have reacted like the disciples on the road to Emmaus. They would have been profoundly disappointed and disillusioned. They would have continued to try to be good Jews and live their lives the best they could, trying to make sense of the three years spent with the "great prophet," Jesus of Nazareth. They certainly would not have made up stories about Jesus' miracles and, finally, his resurrection and then spread these lies so they could be persecuted and, in many cases, tortured and killed.

Indeed, some authors have proposed that one can describe Jesus in one of three ways based on his life and teaching. He is either a lunatic, a liar, or the Lord. After doing research, but most importantly, after reading the Gospels with an open heart, I've concluded that he is the Lord.

If you have questions or doubts about the Gospels and wonder just what you should make of them, don't stop there. Do your research. Read the New Testament and what credible scholars have to say about it. Make sure you seek reliable sources. A lot has been written on the subject. I suggest you ask someone you trust to recommend some good articles and books that will help you get the answers you seek. Your knowledge of the Gospels will open your eyes to the incredible love God has for you and all his people. It will also enable you to open your heart to that divine love and draw you into a profound love affair with our Lord.

Affectionately,
Grandpa

Three | The Catholic Church

My Dear Grandchildren,

Having accepted the reliability and truth of the Gospels, I have become a follower of Jesus Christ. And in doing so, I've become a member of the Church he founded, the Holy Catholic Church. Of course, I was baptized into the Catholic Church as an infant. But I had to make the Faith my own as an adult. And you do too.

I'm sure you know many other Christians who are not Catholic. Many of these non-Catholic Christians are an inspiration in their zeal and love for our Lord. These people have a deep faith. Nevertheless, they are missing so much. They are missing the sacraments and the benefit of the teaching of the Catholic Church in many areas. We need to pray for them. We need to pray for Christian unity.

Our Lord founded his Church and established Peter as its head. "And I tell you, you are Peter, and on this rock I will build my church, and the powers of death shall not prevail against it. I will give you the keys of the kingdom of heaven, and whatever you bind on earth shall be bound in heaven, and whatever you loose on earth shall be loosed in heaven" (Mt 16:18–19).

Indeed, Jesus prayed to the Father for unity in his Church. "I do not pray for these only, but also for those who believe in me through their word, that they may all be one; even as thou, Father, art in me, and I in thee, that they also may be in us, so that the world may believe that thou hast sent me" (Jn 17:20–21).

Jesus made his Church hierarchical, with a teaching authority. This was the only way to ensure unity within his Church. Without a teaching authority Christians would interpret Scripture, doctrinal matters, and moral issues any way they pleased, resulting in a lack of unity. And of course, this is exactly what we have today with a proliferation of Christian denominations, each believing different things about doctrine and morals.

From the earliest days of Christianity, there were attempts to change or misrepresent the teachings of the Gospels and the apostles. We see this clearly in the letters of St. Paul. Writing to the Galatians, Paul said, "I am astonished that you are so quickly deserting him who called you in the grace of Christ and turning to a different gospel—not that there is another gospel, but there are some who trouble you and want to pervert the gospel of Christ" (Gal 1:6–7; also see 2 Cor 11:1–15; Col 2:8; and 1 Tm 1:3–7). So the unity of the Church has been under attack from the beginning. Indeed, the current state of disunity in Christendom is a scandal that undermines the apostolic efficacy of all of Christendom.

No doubt you are aware of the horrible scandals that have plagued the Church for a number of years. We now know that there have been many bishops and priests who have taken advantage of children and others in their care and abused them terribly. This, of course, is an outrage and has led to great suffering on the part of those abused and their families. And it has been the source of immense sadness and anger among faithful Catholics, laity and clergy alike. Clearly, these priests and bishops should never have been accepted into the priesthood in the first place.

These scandals have been faith-shaking events for many Catholics. Indeed, many have walked away from the Church as a result. Unfortunately, these disillusioned Catholics have thrown the baby out with the bathwater. I hope you won't make this mistake too.

We have to remind ourselves of the reason we are Catholics. It should have nothing to do with the existence of virtuous popes, bishops, or priests. While they might inspire us, we are not followers of Fr. so-and-so or Bishop so-and-so or even the holiest of popes. We are followers of Jesus Christ! We are Catholics because we believe Jesus founded our Church and gave us the sacraments to nourish us during our pilgrimage through life. Where else can we witness the unbloody re-presentation of Christ's sacrifice on Calvary in the

Holy Mass? Where else can we be nourished by his Body, Blood, soul, and divinity in Holy Communion? Where else can we be assured of the forgiveness of our sins in the sacrament of confession? Scandals don't change this fundamental reality. Bad priests, bishops, and popes do not change this. Why would we ever walk away from the Church and these incredible gifts?

Some people will cite evil things that people in the Church have done over the past two thousand years. No doubt evil has been done by some churchmen and others in the Church. The Church is both human and divine. Indeed, the Church is for sinners like you and me. We shouldn't be surprised to learn that some people in the Church have done and continue to do terrible things. Nevertheless, in spite of that, history shows that on balance the Catholic Church has been a force for tremendous good since the beginning. There are many books that document this. In fact, modern scholarship shows that the Church—rather than being the intolerant obstacle to progress critics allege—has actually made substantial contributions to Western civilization.

So why am I a Catholic? I'm a Catholic because I believe it is the Church founded by Jesus Christ. I'm a Catholic because I'm a sinner who needs the sacraments. I need to avail myself of the sacrament of mercy regularly. I need the spiritual nourishment provided by the Eucharist each day. And I need the motherly guidance and care that the Church offers me as I make my way through a world full of snares and obstacles.

The Church has been described as a "field hospital for sinners." It's sinners helping other sinners. So we shouldn't be surprised to find evil within the Church. But the Church is also divine. Though his ways can be mysterious, God is guiding his Church. And any thoughtful, fair-minded person can see the profound good the Church has done over the centuries. I hope you will view the Catholic Church as a loving mother who has and continues to bestow on you life-sustaining gifts despite her human frailties.

Affectionately,
Grandpa

Four | Your Sanctity

My Dear Grandchildren,

My life story will probably never appear in any book on the lives of the saints. I really don't expect to be canonized, although, I must say, that is my goal. Every day I struggle to overcome my defects and try to grow in the virtues. I don't get discouraged. Rather, I take great consolation in Jesus' words proclaiming that "I have not come to call the righteous, but sinners to repentance" (Lk 5:32). Jesus sought out sinners for their friendship. So, I fit right in.

Please, don't ever get discouraged by your sinfulness. When we fall, we can go to the sacrament of mercy, where we unburden our souls and seek our Lord's forgiveness, which he readily gives.

As followers of Christ, which is exactly what we are as Christians, we must take the message of the Gospels to heart. The Son of God did not become man, spend about three years of his life teaching us to become holy, and then suffer and die an excruciating death on the cross so we can be mediocre Christians.

Jesus reaches out to us and invites us to be his friend. Have we really accepted his invitation? Our friendship with Christ can never really occur unless we have a relationship with him. The only way we can have a relationship with him is to communicate with him. In other words, we have to pray. We have to converse with him. And because he is not simply *a* friend, but *the* friend, we have to center our lives on him. He made this very clear to us. He said, "I am the way, and the truth, and the life; no one comes to the Father, but by me" (Jn 14:6). Of course, this doesn't necessarily mean that we all have to live in a monastery. Jesus offers his friendship to everyone—students, husbands, wives, single people, priests, and nuns.

When I was a young man in college, I didn't have much of a prayer life at all. In fact, I wandered from the Faith for several years. Even so, I recall admiring Muslims whom I saw taking time out during the day to pray. I never for a minute considered converting to Islam. But it seemed to me that they had something right. To me, they appeared to be living their faith. It just made sense. It appeared to be consistent. This is probably why the teaching of St. Josemaría Escrivá appealed to me when I was introduced to Opus Dei early in my marriage.

St. Josemaría Escrivá taught that everyone is called to holiness, including the laity. Of course, this is totally consistent with the gospel message. But that message seemed to be forgotten for a long time prior to St. Josemaría's emergence on the scene. And, of course, this universal call to holiness was ultimately taught at the Second Vatican Council and is now widely understood, although not widely practiced.

So, you are called to be a saint! And what does this mean in practical terms? It can't just be a pious platitude that sounds good in the company of priests and nuns. Jesus didn't suffer the agony of the Cross for pious platitudes! It means fostering a deep friendship with our Lord. It means struggling to overcome our defects and vices and grow in the virtues. It means swimming against the current of our culture, saying no to what many are saying yes to and saying yes to what many are saying no to. It means taking the time to converse with God in prayer and getting to know him better by reading the New Testament a few minutes each day. It means frequent reception of the sacraments. And it means trying to maintain a sense of the presence of God throughout the day and offering your work and leisure to God as a prayer.

This quest for holiness sounds a bit daunting, doesn't it? But don't worry. No one becomes a saint overnight. We pursue this goal one step at a time with the help of a good spiritual guide. Find a good priest or someone with experience guiding souls to help you along. This made a big difference for me. I started getting together with a priest on a regular basis to discuss my spiritual life. He suggested a plan that I could follow each day to ramp up my prayer life and address some of the defects that were keeping me from growing closer to our Lord. Every couple of weeks we'd meet and talk about how I was doing. Sometimes we'd make some adjustments to my plan based on my struggles and circumstances. I was so grateful for his guidance.

Try to adopt a sporting spirit in the conduct of your spiritual life. You'll win some and you'll lose some. But you'll keep up the struggle with a big smile on your face. Your efforts to be a saint should not lead to a dour existence. Rather, they should be a great source of joy and satisfaction. They won't preclude fun and happy times. You'll continue to play sports and music and pursue hobbies. And you'll have wonderful friends. Your love for Christ will overflow into your relationships with your friends in a very natural way. They'll want to know the source of your joy, and you can tell them.

I'm not suggesting you become a "holy roller." I'm suggesting you be consistent. Are you a follower of Christ or not? For those of us with a lay vocation, we are called to live in the middle of the world just like everyone else. We pursue careers, get married, have families, participate in community activities, and have lots of friends. And we do all this while being steeped in Christ. We are simply called to be great lovers—lovers of God, our families, our friends and colleagues. In many ways, we are called to be revolutionaries. I don't know about you, but I've found it to be quite exciting being a revolutionary in a world that is increasingly confused and too eager to compromise the truth.

Affectionately,
Grandpa

Five | Natural Law

My Dear Grandchildren,

I'm sure you hang around with guys and girls from many different backgrounds and worldviews. Some are Catholic, others are Protestant, some may not be Christian, while some may not embrace any particular faith. This is fine. As friends, you should be able to enjoy many activities together and discuss all kinds of topics, including religion. The common denominator among you and your friends is that you are all children of God. Although you may not share the same faith, you all share a moral law that has been written on the hearts of everyone.

The human being is an incredible creature. And, of course, we were meant to be so, having been created in the image and likeness of God. God created us to be happy, to have lives that are filled with meaning and purpose. But in order for us to reach our potential and be truly happy, we have to live our lives in a way that is intended by our Creator.

A reasonably good analogy is the lawnmower. When we purchase a new lawnmower, we assemble it according to the directions provided in the box by the manufacturer. We place the wheels on the designated axles, we install the handles and the throttle in the correct locations. Finally, we pour the motor oil in the designated place and then fill the gas tank with gasoline. We follow these directions because the manufacturer of the lawnmower knows, we assume, the proper way to assemble the parts along with the correct lubrication and fuel to ensure that the lawnmower will operate the way it is intended. We might consider, for example, if we decided in our wisdom to install only three wheels or to put olive oil where the motor oil is supposed to go—or what if we filled the gas tank with milk instead of gasoline, what would be the result? It's pretty obvious that if we followed our whims rather than the manufacturer's instructions, we wouldn't be cutting much grass. The lawnmower simply would not operate in the manner intended by its manufacturer.

The manufacturer's owner's manual for human beings is the natural moral law. The natural law is articulated in the Ten Commandments. However, it's not a law that applies only to people of certain religions, like Christians and Jews. The natural law applies to all people of all faiths, of all cultures, of all times. Generally, when we break the natural law bad things happen. For example, when we lie or steal, we lose people's trust. When we have sex outside of marriage, we risk the possibility of contracting a disease or conceiving a child that we are not prepared to care for. When we kill an innocent person, we cause great sorrow and hardship for that person's loved ones. You get the idea. There is a natural law that is written on our hearts by our Creator. This law is not constraining any more than the lawnmower manufacturer's operating instructions are constraining. They are provided to enable us to live our lives as our Creator intended. They are provided to make us happy!

Some people might try to convince you that the natural law is conditioned by our cultural norms, that it is not unchanging for all people. However, the notion that a natural law governs our behavior and determines what is morally right and wrong is a pre-Christian concept that has been embraced by a broad spectrum of cultures over a period of centuries, indeed millennia. In its discussion of the natural moral law, the *Catechism of the Catholic Church* cites the Roman philosopher and statesman Cicero, lending credence to the view that natural law is written on the heart of everyone and can be known by unaided reason:

> For there is a true law: right reason. It is in conformity with nature, is diffused among all men, and is immutable and eternal; its orders summon to duty; its prohibitions turn away from offense. . . . To replace it with a contrary law is a sacrilege;

> failure to apply even one of its provisions is forbidden; no one can abrogate it entirely.[3]

Of course, individuals and even societies can have such a malformed and darkened conscience that gross violations of the natural law can occur for many years or even generations in some societies. A good example of this is the legalization of abortion in the United States and many other countries. In this case a large percentage of the adult population believes that the right to kill an innocent pre-born child, even beyond the point of viability, is a good thing. These people believe that a woman has the right to kill her pre-born child for any reason. This is a horror that we pray will soon come to an end. But even in this situation conscience has its revenge. Many women (and men) become deeply troubled after having procured an abortion. This sin is such a gross violation of the natural law that anyone

3. Cicero, *The Republic*, 3, 22, 33, quoted in *Catechism of the Catholic Church*, 2nd ed. (Washington, DC: Libreria Editrice Vaticana–United States Conference of Catholic Bishops, 2000), 1956.

whose conscience is not utterly disabled has great difficulty coming to terms with the profound wrong they committed.

Some have pointed to civilizations where deviant sexual morality or other practices such as human sacrifice were widely accepted as the norm. This doesn't mean that natural law is a fluid thing that changes over time or across cultures. Rather, it points to the effects of man's fallen nature and our misuse of our freedom. When our conscience is dulled through habitually turning our backs on our Creator, we are capable of the most horrible things imaginable. Denial of the natural law essentially gives us license to do whatever evil we find appealing.

The point of this letter is to encourage you to embrace the natural law as a liberating law that will facilitate your journey through life. Staying on the road provided for your journey will help you to get where you want to go. Going off-road may look appealing at first, but it will inevitably result in you getting stuck in the mud or going off a cliff. God knows what he is doing. Trust him! If you follow the Catholic Church's moral teaching, you can't go wrong.

Affectionately,
Grandpa

Six | Your Sexuality

My Dear Grandchildren,

Have you ever seen a work of art, like a sculpture or a painting, that you truly admired and wished you could produce something similar? Of course, you don't just pick up a chisel or a paintbrush and expect to produce a masterpiece. Becoming an accomplished artist requires extensive training and years of practice. Any attempt at sculpting or painting before you are properly trained results in a work with many flaws that is not suitable for display. In many ways, sex is like the work of an artist. We have to prepare ourselves for sex. This preparation involves growing in maturity and self-knowledge and reaching the point in our lives when we can make a lifelong commitment to another person on our wedding day. Engaging in sex before you've made such a commitment usually leads to very unfortunate results.

One of God's most beautiful and powerful gifts to us is our sexuality. Its beauty and power are clear when you consider its ability to express our love, most intimately, to our spouse, and its role in collaborating with God to create new life. I urge you to reflect on these two aspects of our sexuality. Ponder the deep meaning of the marital act. It's rather mind-boggling to consider the responsibility God has given us to cooperate with him in bringing new life into the world.

The topic of sex is a tough issue. In fact, no one likes talking about sex. That includes me. But the world is pushing some very dangerous ideas about sex and I would like to help you avoid much of the pain that falling prey to these falsehoods would cause. I wish I had been taught the true meaning of our sexuality when I was your age. I was taught the biology of sex without being told the whole truth about why sex is only a good thing within the context of marriage.

I'm sure you've been taught that sex is a gift of self. But what does that really mean? How do I give myself to another person? When we give ourselves to another person, we are essentially saying, "I give myself to you, I'm yours." This is a gift for a lifetime. When we give ourselves to that person, we necessarily hold nothing back. In fact, my gift of myself is so complete that I am prepared to join myself with that person in such a way that the fruit of our union will live on for eternity in the form of another soul.

A commitment like this requires a lot of maturity. We need considerable self-knowledge and to be in a position to start a family. Your wedding day will be the day you announce to the world your commitment to give yourself to your beloved for as long as you both shall live.

Of course, sex is meant to be desirable and it is very good. God made the things that are necessary for sustaining and creating life enjoyable in order to ensure that we will do what needs to be done for the human race to thrive and expand. Think eating and sex. If these activities had no pleasure associated with them, there's a good chance we would forget about eating and fail to reproduce.

Sex is like everything else we do. If we don't heed the moral law or the physical law, bad things tend to happen. Remember the last time you ate too much? The pizza tasted really good going down. But later you suffered the consequences and felt pretty awful. Or have you ever told a lie because you thought it would save you a lot of trouble when, ultimately, you just lost the trust of someone you cared about? Have you ever been in a situation where you felt you were just being used by someone? Maybe someone was just being friendly to you so he could meet someone else through you. Essentially, he was just using you to get what he really wanted. I think we've all experienced something like that at one time or another. It's not a very nice feeling to realize you've been used by someone else. Casual sex between unmarried people is a lot like that. People seeking the pleasure of sex without any commitment may "like" the person with whom they are having sex, but in reality, they are merely using that person for their own sexual gratification. And that person is using them too! Human beings should not be used like an object even if they consent to it. It is simply beneath our dignity as human beings made in the image and likeness of God to use another person or to allow ourselves to be used like an object.

So, as a single person with red blood flowing through your veins and a healthy attraction to the opposite sex, what are you to do? The first thing is to acknowledge that God gave you a sex drive that is meant for good. However, it is meant to be used properly. We are not beasts who act on instinct alone. We have an intellect and a free will. We can control ourselves (contrary to what some will tell you). But we have to be smart and avoid situations that may lead to trouble. It's important to avoid unhelpful material on the Internet—especially pornography. You need to be prudent in your dealings with the opposite sex and not put yourself in difficult situations. Seek out friends who will support you in your desire to foster chaste relationships. And finally, you need to pray. Strive to have a close friendship with our Lord. Everyone needs to struggle to live the virtue of chastity, whether they are single, married, or even a priest or a nun. You are not alone in this struggle. Pray for the grace to persevere and frequent the sacraments. Do it for yourself and your future family.

At some point in your life, you will meet people with same-sex attraction. Some may be struggling to live chastely and others may be involved in a homosexual lifestyle. I've known a number of gay men over the years. Most I've encountered in the workplace. Back in my twenties, I was somewhat friendly with one gay coworker. I had trouble getting too close to him since he was very much into the gay lifestyle. If I had been more mature and gotten advice from a priest or someone I trust, I probably could have become better friends with him. Maybe I could have helped him.

As I'm sure you know, homosexuality is nothing new; reports of homosexuality date back thousands of years. St. Paul condemns homosexual activity at the beginning of the Christian age (see Rom 1:26–28, 32). It seems there is little agreement as to its cause and the ability of one with same-sex attraction to reverse this inclination. Nevertheless, the Church is clear in its teaching that while same-sex attraction is not inherently sinful, engaging in homosexual acts is gravely sinful because sex outside of marriage is a serious sin. You see, sex outside of marriage is sinful for both homosexual and heterosexual people. It is a violation of the natural law.

The Church also makes it clear that while the homosexual condition is disordered, those with this condition deserve our respect and should be treated with charity and not be discriminated against. Rather, they should be treated with compassion; for many with this condition, their suffering is a cross that can be united to the Cross of Christ.

All Christians are called to live chastely within their state in life. Homosexuals too, despite their particular burden, are called to a life of chastity, supported by a life of prayer and sacramental grace.

I know it takes courage, but it is a mistake to approve or legally recognize same-sex unions. It undermines the institution of marriage by introducing profound confusion regarding its meaning and purpose. It robs your friends who struggle with this teaching the opportunity to hear the truth about what marriage really is because it is rarely understood or spoken of today.

It may be helpful to consider the human body and the functions of its various parts. We have hands and fingers for grasping things; our eyes enable us to see; our teeth are for chewing food. Most everything in our bodies has a purpose. Of course, we can misuse our bodily parts. For example, we can use our hands and fingers to punch an innocent person or poke an eye out. We are free to use our bodies as they are meant to be used, or we can misuse them and injure ourselves or someone else. We are free to use our bodies for good and evil. We also have reproductive organs. However, these reproductive organs are unable to result in reproduction unless a man and a woman unite in sexual intercourse. Reproduction can't occur through the sexual embrace of two men or two women. It must be a man and a woman. So sexual activity clearly has a purpose as well. It's a purpose ordained by God, our Creator. It's pretty hard to get around this fact. Sex is for making babies! Of course, it's also for expressing the love of a husband and wife. If we consider these two purposes of sex, it becomes pretty clear that sex is only appropriate within marriage. It's only within the permanency of a marriage that a child can be raised by his or her mother and father until he or she reaches adulthood. Homosexual sex is, by its nature, infertile. It is a misuse of our sexual function.

Some same-sex couples may wish to adopt children; however, this would be a gross injustice to the children, who would be denied a mother or a father. There is plenty of research that shows that both mothers and fathers make different contributions to the parenting dynamic that children need to flourish. It would also be wrong to place adoptive children with parents whose relationship is inherently immoral.

In today's society holding and expressing these views about homosexuality and same-sex marriage will lead to you being called a bigot or a hater or a homophobe. Don't be intimidated by this name-calling. Of course, nothing is further from the truth. You have to love, respect, and support those with same-sex attraction while holding on to the truth about marriage and our sexuality. This will require courage on your part. You can help your friends understand these truths and maybe little by little our society will again embrace the truth about marriage and our sexuality.

I know this is a lot to digest. I urge you to reflect on this prayerfully. I have to tell you that my marriage to Grandma has been a wonderful adventure. I can't begin to express the joy we've experienced spending our lives together and raising our family despite the many challenges we've had to face. I can assure you that struggling to live chastely now and throughout your life will magnify the joy you have in store for you whatever your vocation may be.

Affectionately,
Grandpa

Seven | Family

My Dear Grandchildren,

Reflecting on family and family life after seventy years of life, I have a perspective that you could not have at this point in your life. So I'll share that perspective with you and encourage you to take it to heart and consider it as you navigate the sometimes-turbulent waters of your own family life.

Your nuclear family (Mom and Dad, brothers, and sisters) help provide you with an identity that should be a great source of security and peace. This is the school of love in which you are meant to thrive.

Your mother and father love you with a love that you cannot possibly understand until you yourself are a parent. I remember when your grandmother and I were expecting our first child. I was in graduate school at the time, and we were excited and filled with anticipation. I'm not sure I can fully describe the feeling. My life would never be the same. When he was born, I experienced a certain vulnerability. I felt my heart might explode. This wasn't just a function of experiencing something new. The love of a child has a character that is different from the love of anyone else. Regardless of the number of children we have, each child is unrepeatable and is the object of a unique love. And this love persists all our life. Remember this love is there in spite of the struggles your mom and dad have to be good parents. They're not perfect. They have defects just like you. So try to be patient with them when they lose their temper or seem not to listen or when you feel they simply don't understand you. They're trying. And remember that they love you more deeply than you can possibly grasp.

Although it may not always seem like it, your siblings are gifts from God. They truly are. They've been given to you to be your companions at home. And you have been given to each other to look out for each other outside of your home. They've also been given to you to help you to grow in virtue. They provide you with opportunities to grow in patience and generosity. Living in a family with your brothers and sisters provides the setting for truly learning how to love. Love is a choice. It's not a feeling. We know that our love is real when it's sacrificial. When we love someone, we give of ourselves. So, when you cheerfully put up with an annoying brother or sister and treat him or her with kindness even though you might like to do something quite different, that's loving!

I have an older brother and sister and a younger sister and two younger brothers. I was closest to my younger sister because we were closest in age and shared many friends growing up. Thankfully, we have all remained close and try to stay in touch despite being rather spread out geographically. Even now, we all try to get together once a year for a siblings' reunion. I treasure the relationships I have with my brothers and sisters and continue to pray for them every day.

You may not realize it now, but your brothers and sisters are destined to become your best friends. You will always care for one another and be there when they need help regardless of how far you live from each other. These family bonds are a treasure that many people underestimate. However, like any relationship, family relationships require a certain amount of effort. They require communication. You need to make the effort to stay in touch. Try to foster friendships with your brothers and sisters. Keep the phone calls and emails flowing. Make the effort to have family gatherings and one-on-one get-togethers.

As a parent, it warms my heart to see that my adult children are such good friends with each other. They provide each other with support, companionship, and camaraderie all the time. Seeing that they care so much for each other provides me with such comfort. I know that when their mother and I are gone they will still have each other come thick or thin. That's the way it's supposed to be.

Your extended family can also be a wonderful source of support and friendship. If you're fortunate enough to live near your cousins, try to foster close relationships with them. Hopefully, this would have begun while you were very young. Nevertheless, it will behoove you to make the effort to spend time with your cousins. They too are family and can become as close as brothers and sisters if you nurture those relationships. They can become lifelong friends who will enrich your life incredibly.

I urge you to see your family as the treasure that it is. Try to look beyond the transitory frictions and annoyances that inevitably crop up in family life. This will happen under the best of circumstances. And if your family is not the school of love that it is supposed to be, take it upon yourself to pray that it become so. Maybe you can provide the example to the others and show them how to love with the love of Christ. Your family members ought to be the first focus of your prayer. Don't restrict your prayer to those occasions when there are hard times. Your family needs your prayer even when things are going well. Pray especially for your parents. Your mom and dad have a tough job. They have a lot of responsibility. Your prayers will help them a lot.

Finally, you might think of yourself as an apostle in the family. Strive to bring your brothers and sisters closer to our Lord—especially if you have younger siblings. Your younger brothers and sisters look up to you. Without being pushy, through your example and occasional words of encouragement you can help your younger siblings to deepen their faith and grow closer to Jesus. You can make a big difference in their lives if you take the trouble to care.

Affectionately,
Grandpa

Eight | Vocation

My Dear Grandchildren,

God our Lord has a plan for each person he creates: his or her sanctity. Within this universal Christian vocation to holiness, he has a specific plan for each of us. You will discover this calling if you develop a personal relationship with Christ.

Pope Francis addressed these words to young people: "Jesus looks at you and invites you to go with Him. Dear young people, have you noticed this look towards you? Have you heard this voice? Have you felt this urge to undertake this journey?" A personal encounter with Jesus can be difficult to achieve today, with "the noise and confusion seemingly prevalent in the world." Nevertheless, "this call continues to resonate in the depths of your heart so as to open it to joy in its fullness." It will be possible to achieve this, the pope says, with "professional guides" from whom "you will learn how to undertake a journey of discernment to discover God's plan in your life."[4]

We are all called to a specific vocation by God. You too have a vocation, and it's vitally important that you spend these years trying to discern your vocation. Our Lord may be calling you to married life or possibly to the priesthood or religious life or to apostolic celibacy. These are all divine vocations and they may all be attractive to you. It's your job to figure out what it is that God is calling you to. This can only be done if you have a life of prayer. You don't have to enter a monastery to do this. Just take some

---

4. Pope Francis, Letter to Young People on the Occasion of the Presentation of the *Preparatory Document* of the 15th Ordinary General Assembly of the Synod of Bishops (January 13, 2017) Vatican website: www.vatican.va.

time each day to converse with our Lord. Listen to him. Ask him directly, "Lord, what do you want from me?" Try not to be distracted by what might appeal to you. A good priest or nun or dedicated lay person should find the idea of married life appealing. It's a very good thing! No one should embrace apostolic celibacy because they were not attracted to married life, but because they believe God has given them the gift of that vocation and they choose to respond generously, giving their whole life to serving God exclusively.

All vocations come with tremendous blessings and considerable challenges—our Lord invited us to pick up our cross daily and follow him. In married life we have the companionship of a husband or wife and the blessing of cooperating with God in the creation of new life. Raising a family comes with many joys and sometimes great heartaches. We have the joy of forming our children into fine Catholic adults. But we may also have to deal with financial problems and health issues and children who make bad decisions that can seriously complicate their lives.

Priests are blessed with the joy of being spiritual fathers to many souls. They have the privilege of acting in the person of Christ while saying Holy Mass and hearing confessions. Through the power of Jesus' words uttered by the priest, our Savior's Body, Blood, soul, and divinity become a reality in the hands of the priest. And again, our Lord works through the priest to forgive the sins of anyone who approaches him in the sacrament of confession. It is Jesus who forgives the sins and it is Jesus to whom we confess, regardless of the virtues of the priest. To say the Mass and unburden souls are profound blessings for priests. Nevertheless, they go without the joy of family life and their lives can be lonely at times.

Nuns dedicate their lives as brides of Christ, serving the Church and the people of God. The life of a nun will vary considerably depending on the order to which she is called. A nun living out her vocation is filled with joy as she pursues God's will for her. No doubt there are also trials associated with religious life and living in community with other sisters. And those laity called to apostolic celibacy will lay down their lives to serve Christ in their brothers and sisters within their spiritual family, and they will spend themselves laboring in his vineyard for the salvation and sanctification of all souls.

Regardless of the vocation to which you are called, you will have a life of joy and sacrifice. Apparently, St. Teresa of Ávila described life as "a bad night in a bad inn." While that may sound overly pessimistic, it's important to keep in mind that St. Teresa was filled with joy. The joy of knowing that we are children of God and destined for heaven will get us through all kinds of adversity. If we seek God's will for us and struggle to live according to his will day in and day out, life will be truly rewarding, come what may.

Certain occupations are frequently referred to as vocations, and in some sense they may be. Some people may believe that they have a calling to be a teacher or a social worker. Or you may feel called to be an artist or a musician or a doctor. These, like many others, are noble professions, and if you feel drawn to a particular line of work, then get the education and training needed to pursue it. However, it's important to keep in mind that these are, in fact, just jobs and they must be compatible with the divine vocation to which you've been called. If your dream job is incompatible with your vocation to marriage and raising a family, you should consider an alternative. For example, your art or music may need to be relegated to a hobby while you pursue a line of work that enables you to support a family.

In closing, I urge you to reflect on the notion of vocation. Make good use of these years to foster your generosity to say YES to God and to discern just what he has in mind for you. Take it to your prayer frequently. Find a good spiritual advisor to guide you. Your parents and perhaps one of your teachers can help you see more clearly where our Lord is guiding you. Try to keep an open mind. God knows you better than you know yourself. Trust him! He knows how to make you happy.

Affectionately,
Grandpa

Nine | Friendships

My Dear Grandchildren,

Your friendships are among your most treasured possessions in life. Cultivate them and nurture them. Your friendships will enrich your life. Remember that true friends share what they value most in life and care about each other's well-being. More than a buddy, a true friend wants what is best for you. He or she wants you to be happy, to have a good life, and to be the best person you can be.

Some people have a harder time than others making friends. It's not their fault. It's just the way they were made. Some of us have a more introverted personality. However, by making the effort to meet people and getting to know them, your circle of friends will expand and your life will become more interesting. Of course, you will not be close friends with everyone you know. You will have a few close friends, some more distant friends, and many acquaintances.

Take an interest in the people you meet—at parties, school, work, in the neighborhood. Ask them about themselves. Find out about their interests, hobbies, where they work, where they go to school, what they want to do when they finish school. People generally like talking about themselves. A potential friend will, at some point, turn the conversation to you. He or she will want to learn more about you. You would be amazed at how many times I've been at cocktail parties and struck up a conversation with someone I didn't know and when the conversation was over, I knew all kinds of things about this person and he or she knew absolutely nothing about me. They were simply uninterested in learning anything about me. They clearly were not interested in making a new friend. Oh well, their loss! Right? Dale Carnegie, in his classic *How to Win Friends and Influence People*, said, "You can make more friends in two months by becoming interested in other people than you can in two years by trying to get other people interested in you."

Like any relationship, cultivating and maintaining a friendship takes a certain amount of effort. We invest in a friendship. We need to communicate with our friends and spend time with them. Take the initiative in arranging get-togethers and outings. Those common experiences will cement the relationship like nothing else. As friends, we need to be there when they have problems and when they need help. We help them move into a new apartment even though it's a big inconvenience. We listen to them when they need to talk. And we correct them when they need correcting. And we are ready to accept their corrections.

If we are truly friends, we are duty bound to charitably correct our friends when needed. For example, if we witnessed a friend being rude or inconsiderate to someone, as a loyal friend we would point it out to him or her. It would be wise to talk to your friend alone, calmly and diplomatically, but without sugarcoating the behavior. Even if he or she doesn't take it well initially, you will have done your friend a great service. A more difficult situation would be if your friend had an unhealthy relationship with another person. This is an area we would need to get advice on and to pray about. An unhealthy relationship can have life-altering consequences, so it's important that we be proactive. In these situations, you need to have an empathetic but frank conversation with your friend, pointing out the dangers. You will discern how best to approach your friend tactfully, but you will need to be clear that you're pointing out the problem because of your concern for your friend's well-being.

Of course, we need to be open to receiving corrections too. For most people, it's not easy giving a friend a correction. We don't know how it will be received. Will they get angry? Will we hurt their feelings? So we should try to keep this in mind when we are corrected. It's good form to thank our friend for pointing out the issue to us.

We don't need friends in an echo chamber who just tell us what we want to hear. We know we are all a work in progress, so we should be grateful for a piece of positive advice from a friend. Friendships can and should survive differences of opinion. Indeed, we can have great friendships with people of different faiths and political persuasions. The ancient Greek author and philosopher Plutarch famously said, "I don't need a friend who changes when I change and who nods when I nod; my shadow does that much better."[5]

Much of the time you spend with your friends will involve studying together and light entertainment—sports, outdoor activities like hiking or camping, concerts, and so on. That's to be encouraged. But, don't be afraid to take your friendship to a deeper level, discussing things that really matter, things about which you may disagree. A good friendly debate can be a wonderful thing as long as it's done in a calm,

---

5. Plutarch, Essay, "How to Tell a Flatterer from a Friend," *Moralia.*

respectful manner. Share your dreams and fears with your friends. It's not a friendship if you can't expose your heart a bit. When we love someone, we open our heart and make ourselves somewhat vulnerable. Of course, it's a risk. But it's a risk worth taking. We have to be prudent. We don't bare our soul to just anyone. But our close friends are special. We know them well and they know us well.

So, I urge you to make the effort to expand your circle of friends. Your life will be richer and more interesting if you do. And keep in mind that if we want what is best for our friends, we want them to grow closer to our Lord. Keep your friends in your prayers. You know what they need. Storm heaven for them! Don't be afraid to talk about God and share your faith with them. You want your friends to be happy in this life and especially for all eternity.

Affectionately,
Grandpa

Ten | The Poor

My Dear Grandchildren,

Does our contact with poor people sometimes make us feel uncomfortable? This may be because the poor remind us of just how well-off we are and how ungrateful and ungenerous we can be. We all can easily take for granted our incredible blessings. We have to make a point of seeing Jesus in the face of the poor. Remember, he said, "Truly, I say to you, as you did it to one of the least of these my brethren, you did it to me" (Mt 25:40).

My first face-to-face contact with the poor took place in Panama as a teenager. My family moved to the Panama Canal Zone because my father took a job as a Panama Canal pilot. There I saw both children and adults without shoes, wearing tattered clothes and begging on the streets. I saw similar sights in Mexico when I was studying Spanish there during graduate school, and again more recently on a mission trip to Jamaica. Of course, there is poverty everywhere you go, even in the United States and other developed countries.

It makes us wonder, why? Why is there such poverty in the world alongside such tremendous wealth? Many politicians and activists over the years have campaigned to eliminate poverty. Yet as we look around us, we can see that the poor are still with us to varying degrees. It seems the existence of poverty is a fact of life. And while we work to alleviate the needs of others when and where we can, the poor we encounter can move our hearts to be more generous, compassionate, and less attached to our things, our little luxuries.

It may be that God wants us to reach out to the poor in some way to help. Maybe we can just give a poor, homeless person a smile and a word of acknowledgement that he too is made in the image and likeness of God and has great worth—or maybe you could even buy him a sandwich. Maybe you could get involved in a parish project to distribute food or visit the elderly. There are opportunities for some young people to participate in work camps in the summertime repairing homes. The poor give us a wonderful opportunity to get outside of ourselves and our own concerns and take an interest in the well-being of those less fortunate. It's a great opportunity for growth. It's Jesus who is calling us to grow by ministering to him through his poor. And, of course, we can and should pray for the poor and express our thanks to God for all the blessings we have.

We are all called to live a certain spiritual poverty. Jesus said, "Blessed are the poor in spirit, for theirs is the kingdom of heaven" (Mt 5:3). So what does it mean to be poor in spirit? For the laity, it means being detached from material possessions. You may have some things that mean a lot to you—like an item of clothing, a phone, a musical instrument, a cool car. How would you take it if you had to give up one of those items? Or if one of them were damaged? Would it be the end of the world? Would it ruin your life? Or would you express your dismay or disappointment and then move on and make do without it? If it's the latter, then you are detached from your possessions and you are spiritually enriched. You are practicing some semblance of spiritual poverty. If it's the former, you've set your heart on the wrong things—and we were told, "set not your heart on [riches]" (Ps 62:10). Spiritual poverty does not mean you can't enjoy the use of nice things. It does mean you don't have lots of superfluous things, you don't indulge all your cravings, and you're not overly attached to the things you like. If you lose them, you may be disappointed, but you will maintain your cheerful disposition and make do without them.

St. Josemaría Escrivá would tell a story to make this point. There was a poor fellow who would come into a soup kitchen each day. He would sit down at the table with his bowl of soup and then take out a pewter spoon from his pocket. He would look at the spoon admiringly before eating his soup. When he was finished, he would lick the spoon clean, take a moment to gaze at his spoon, wrap it in a piece of cloth, and put it into his pocket again. St. Josemaría would say that this poor beggar did not live poverty, due to his attachment to his precious spoon. On the other hand, there was a rich widow who was extraordinarily generous. She cheerfully gave away much of her wealth and was very generous with her time. She thought little of her own needs. The saint described this widow as being truly poor in spirit due to her total detachment from her material possessions.

Another aspect of living a spirit of poverty is taking good care of your things so they will last. If you have a lackadaisical attitude about taking care of your things, thinking, "If it breaks, I'll just get a new one," this would be counter to a spirit of poverty. Ensuring that your car or other things get regular maintenance will help them last a long time and continue to operate properly. Such care will allow us to use our money on other things, such as contributing to a charity, rather than purchasing a replacement earlier than we otherwise would.

So we can consider the poor in our society as a gift to us from God. It's up to us to accept this gift by caring for them in any way we can. You probably don't have much money available for donating to the poor, though you may have some. But you certainly can carve out some time for volunteering and helping the needy in some way. There may be someone in your neighborhood who is lonely, an elderly person who would love to have a visit from you from time to time. And remember to smile and greet the poor fellow on the corner asking for a handout. You may not have money to give him, or perhaps you can only give him a little, but you can certainly give him the respect he deserves as a child of God.

Finally, a recurring topic of our prayer should be offering thanksgiving to God for all our blessings. Everything we have, both material and spiritual, is a gift from God. Thank him. Ask him to help you be more detached from all that you have and to be more generous to those in need. And ask him to help you see how you can minister to him through his poor.

Affectionately,
Grandpa

Eleven | Work

My Dear Grandchildren,

We were placed on this earth to work! Some people think that the need to work is a consequence of original sin. If only Adam and Eve hadn't ruined everything by their disobedience, we'd all have it made living a life of leisure every day! However, that isn't the case. Prior to the Fall, God called man to till the earth and keep it (see Gn 2:15). Work was always part of the deal. So, rather than shunning work, try to embrace it as an integral aspect of the human condition.

There are different types of work. There's manual labor. There's intellectual work. There's also domestic work, caring for children, the elderly, and the infirm. Of course, these types of work can overlap in many ways. For example, certain types of manual labor can have an intellectual element requiring calculations, measurements, and the like. A student is also engaged in work. His or her studies entail attending classes, reading, conducting experiments, practicing math problems, and studying.

Why should work be an integral part of the human condition? Clearly, it is God's intention that man should work. In addition to Scripture pointing to this fact, we see this in everyday life. Anyone who has been unemployed for any length of time knows how dehumanizing this situation can be. People need to work. It gives them a sense of worth. We all need to know that we are contributing in some way to society.

Not all work brings great human satisfaction to everyone engaged in it. Some of us have jobs that we don't particularly like. However, we continue to work at that job in order to make a living and support our family. In these situations, we may look to other activities to provide the satisfaction we desire. I spent my career working as an economist, mostly in the federal government. I liked the work well enough and finished my career as the chief economist for a small government agency. However, it didn't provide me with the creative outlet I needed. I filled that need by working on the side, in my spare time, writing books on fatherhood and Catholic apologetics. The book you're reading is the product of that need.

There is a spiritual element to work as well. All noble work, whether it entails menial labor such as picking up trash on the sidewalk or working to discover a cure for cancer, can be offered to God as a prayer. Any offering to God must be high quality. It has to be the best that we can do. Shoddy work could never be an appropriate offering to God. Indeed, St. Josemaría taught that the work of the most value is that which is done with the most love.

If you are a student, this means making a morning offering first thing in the morning, offering your day to God. It means taking your studies seriously (even the courses you're not too interested in) and giving them your best effort.

We all have to do certain tasks that are not particularly appealing. For you it may mean doing some chores around the house. No one likes doing dishes, weeding the garden, doing the laundry, or picking up their room. This too is work and these tasks can be sanctified. They can be offered to God as a prayer. How can you possibly convert mundane tasks like doing the dishes into a prayer? It's really quite simple. Do it cheerfully, even though you don't feel particularly cheerful. Do the best job you can. And offer that job to God. You may have an intention for which to offer your work on this unpleasant job. You could offer those dishes or that weeding for your friend who is going through a tough time. Or offer them for your sick uncle or for the Church or your country.

So, doing jobs that you find unpleasant can be a form of penance for our sins. Our Lord asked us to "deny ourselves." The spiritual writers call self-denial mortification and describe it as the prayer of the senses. This can take many different forms: fasting, eating foods we don't like, not eating foods we do like, enduring some discomfort like heat or cold for a period of time, or cleaning our bedroom without being asked to do so. These things become mortifications (dying to ourselves) when they take on a supernatural objective. We cheerfully endure unpleasantness so we can identify with the Cross of Christ. He said that we must carry our cross daily, if we are to follow him. This is how we can do it voluntarily.

It's helpful to think of your work as a form of service. All noble work is cooperating with God in his ongoing creative work. Your work, no matter how mundane, is God's work if done well, with love and as an offering to our Lord.

Your studies are a preparation for a life of work. Your classes are designed to teach you to reason and solve problems. They help you to better understand the culture and history of civilization. Some of your classes will have a direct application to your future profession. Others may seem to be less relevant. Your work as a student is to prepare yourself as best you can. This is your job.

It's important that you seek an appropriate balance in your life. Your work or your studies should not completely displace your time with your family and friends. In addition to your work you have family obligations, duties around the house, as well as family time. Of course, your prayer life should not suffer due to confused priorities. If you are using your time well, you should have time to devote to your work or studies, family, and prayer life. Granted, there will be times when you have a big deadline or you're preparing for exams when most of your time is devoted to your work or your studies. However, your life should normally be in balance. If you are finding that your life is out of balance, look at how you are using your time. There's a good chance you are wasting your time in some way—too much TV, too much screen time, too much sleep.

Remember that your time is a treasure! We are all tempted to think that we have plenty of time to accomplish all of our goals. But life is short! Believe me, though it may not seem like it to you now, eighty or even ninety years will go by quickly. Use your time well.

That doesn't mean you can't enjoy life and have fun. Just don't waste your time. You were put on this earth for a purpose. God is expecting big things from you.

Affectionately,
Grandpa

Twelve | Leisure

My Dear Grandchildren,

Even though work is meant to be an integral part of our lives, it's not meant to absorb all of our lives. Indeed, our work should be a means to an end, not the end itself. We need leisure time in our lives in order to fully flourish. Leisure enables us to take in God's creation and appreciate its beauty. Our work should facilitate our leisure time. If we find that our work is usurping our leisure, there is an imbalance in our life and we need to correct it. Granted, there will be times when our work is all-consuming. This, however, should be an exception. This is true whether we are married or single.

It is important to distinguish between work, amusement, and leisure. John Cuddeback, professor of philosophy, says,

> Work is directed to some product outside the activity itself, and so generally it is not done for its own sake. Play or amusement is aimed at pleasant diversion, and in some sense is done for its own sake. Leisure in the proper sense names activities that are done for their own sake because they are intrinsically worth doing. Meditation and a conversation with a friend about higher realities, for example, are especially meaningful activities, and in themselves they constitute a significant enactment of human life.[6]

6. John Cuddeback, *Leisure as the Basis of Home Life*, Ethika Politica, Catholic Culture, https://www.catholicculture.org/culture/library/view.cfm?recnum=11028.

He points out that amusement serves work by refreshing us and enabling us to return to work. And work serves leisure. He says further that,

> It would be silly to live for amusement. It would likewise be silly to live for work. Something other than these provides the reason for it all. So Aristotle has pointed out a hierarchy, holding that all activities find their ultimate purpose in the activities of leisure.

So, our leisure shouldn't be characterized by just doing nothing or mindlessly being plugged into the TV or computer. That's simply amusement. And by all means, don't waste your day by sleeping until noon. Try going for a hike with friends or family in the woods or along a hiking trail near your home. Other outdoor activities such as fishing, hunting, or camping, when done with friends, can provide a wonderful opportunity to deepen friendships and embrace the beauty of God's creation.

Our leisure time is a good time to develop hobbies, learn to play a musical instrument, study a foreign language, or read a good book. Use your leisure time to grow, to learn, to deepen relationships, and to better appreciate the world around you.

Sunday is especially meant for leisure. That usually takes some advanced planning. Try to get your weekend studying done on Saturday. I know that can be a tall order. But we really need to try to disconnect from our work on Sunday, making it truly the Lord's Day for us. Spend the day with family and friends, doing outdoor activities, and making visits to the poor and elderly. Sunday would also be a good day to focus on your spiritual reading and prayer. If you watch sports on Sunday, try to do it with a friend or another family member, making it more of a social event.

When I was in high school, my leisure time was largely spent playing sports and hanging out with my friends. Looking back, my time would have been better served by reading more. These days I enjoy writing, reading, and going on long walks. I also like visiting with my family and friends.

It's always good for us to re-examine how we use our time—particularly how we use our leisure time. Am I mostly just amusing myself with activities of little intrinsic value? Or am I involved in activities that provide meaning to the rest of my life?

Affectionately,
Grandpa

Thirteen | Freedom

My Dear Grandchildren,

We all desire freedom and rightly so. True freedom is a gift from God to enable us to love him and fulfill his will. If we were not free, we would not be capable of loving or serving. Yes, God created us with a free will, unlike the animals, which are driven largely by instinct. We can choose to love God and others or not.

I know you sometimes feel like you have no freedom. Your parents set certain rules that you have to obey. You have to go to school. You must be home by a certain hour in the evening. You're required to do chores at home. Where's the freedom here? Right? Well, it turns out, you are freer than you may think. These constraints set by your parents will enable you to flourish now and in the long-term. Let's consider the idea of freedom and what it means.

When we learn about terrible crimes such as murder or rape, our initial reaction may be asking how God could allow such cruelty to happen. If he is a good God who loves everyone, how could he allow such terrible things? Of course, God does not want anyone to do evil. However, he so respects our freedom, our ability to choose the good or evil, that he allows us to commit evil deeds. Imagine if God had "programmed" us to do only what is good, that is, to only do his will: We would be similar to robots, unable to choose our course of action. Without our freedom we could not truly love God, or anyone else for that matter.

It is important to distinguish between freedom and license. Our freedom enables us to choose the good. This is what we were created for—goodness and truth. Indeed, our Lord said, "I am the way, and the truth, and the life" (Jn 14:6), and "you will know the truth, and the truth will make you free" (Jn 8:32). License amounts to doing whatever we feel like regardless of the consequences or its impact on the good of others. For example, license might lead you to imitate others and use drugs if you so choose, even though they will damage your health and enrich drug dealers who go on to help ruin the lives of many others.

Paradoxically, freedom is consistent with having certain restrictions in our life. Living according to the moral law and avoiding certain behaviors (such as lying, stealing, having sex outside of marriage, and abusing drugs and alcohol) enables us to thrive and reach our potential. To illustrate this point, imagine that you are planning a road trip to a town a few hundred miles away. If you follow the route indicated by a map or GPS, you will arrive at your destination at the expected time. However, if you had a friend traveling in another car who chose to take her car off-road and cut across a grassy field, it's likely that she would get stuck in the mud or damage her car. In this case, who's freer? You, who chose to restrict yourself to the roads specified by the GPS, or your friend, who chose to abandon the highway and cut across the field and is now waiting for a tow truck to pull her back to the highway? It turns out restricting yourself to the roads indicated by the GPS enabled you to arrive at your destination in a timely manner and enjoy the company of the friends you were planning to visit. In the same way, when we choose the good, we enhance our freedom, because it permits our lives to flourish.

When we choose evil, that is, when we sin, we give in to our weaknesses, passions, impulses, and bad habits. And we soon become slaves to these passions, impulses, and habits. Indeed, we become slaves to sin. This is apparent if we have a well-formed conscience. When we give in to our weaknesses and choose to sin, we allow these weaknesses to control us. We become their slave. And we soon regret our actions.

An example of how we can become slaves to sin is the use of pornography. Pornography use is highly addictive. Research has shown that pornography essentially "rewires" the user's brain, making him or her more and more dependent on more explicit and disturbing forms of porn. The porn user becomes its slave—quite literally.

We all have weaknesses and defects that we need to conquer or try to moderate. We may be subject to laziness, impatience, anger, or sensuality. If we don't struggle to overcome these defects, they can take over our lives. Our laziness can impede our ability to accomplish goals we've established for ourselves. It may even prevent us from setting our goals. Our impatience can interfere with our relationships and cause us to experience frustration when our plans don't develop as we expect. Unrestrained sensuality can lead us to degrade our view of those of the opposite sex, cheapening our attitude toward sex, turning it into a selfish pursuit of pleasure. You can see how these weaknesses turn against us, take control, and diminish us. However, if we make a consistent effort to grow in virtue and overcome our defects, we become freer to take control of our lives and become all that God has created us to be.

Remember that your God-given freedom allows you to choose to love God and others despite an environment that pushes you to do otherwise, a pagan environment that is often godless and hostile to a life of holiness. Even if you were physically constrained and imprisoned, you would be interiorly free to love. No one can take that away from you. But you have to make that choice. Choose the good and you will be free to flourish as God intends.

Affectionately,
Grandpa

Fourteen | Education

My Dear Grandchildren,

Being well educated is the best way to advance in the world and to gain a deep appreciation for God's creation. While you are young, I suggest you make your education a priority. Indeed, while you are in school, your studies are your job and, as with any job, you should strive to do them well to make them a worthy offering to God.

At times you may question the value of pursuing your education. You may ask, "When will I actually use the trigonometry I'm studying now?" And really,

"Just how relevant to my life is reading Shakespeare or Dickens?" These are good questions. But keep in mind that your education is much more than learning practical facts. It involves training your mind to think and analyze, skills that you will use for the rest of your life. It also involves acquiring an understanding and an appreciation of our civilization and culture.

Your education should entail so much more than mastering your academic subjects, such as math, chemistry, English literature, history, or Spanish. Strive to dig deeper into your school subjects and expand your horizons through outside reading. I strongly suggest you limit your screen time. Try to discipline yourself to minimize the time you spend on social media. Social media is designed to be addictive, and you can waste many hours a day if you're not careful.

Find a well-educated mentor, maybe a teacher or a friend of the family, and ask him or her to help you put together a good reading list. The list should include both fiction and nonfiction. Don't ignore the classic works of literature. The list should also include good spiritual books. Don't worry if the list seems overwhelming. You may work your way through the list over a number of years—maybe over a lifetime. The important thing is that you have a plan to plow through many good books over a period of time. You might consider forming a book club with some of your friends. Reading and discussing the same books with your friends is a great way to dig more deeply into the books as well as (and maybe more importantly) deepen your friendships.

Your education should entail more than acquiring skills for making a good living. Acquiring such skills is very important, but that's not the same thing as getting educated. Make an effort to learn about music, art, and other cultures. Try to expand your knowledge of history, including the history of other countries. Learning another language can be very enriching, enabling you to converse with people from other countries in their own language. One of my biggest regrets in life is not becoming fluent in Spanish. I studied Spanish and lived in Panama and Puerto Rico but never really got comfortable with the language. I can't help but think that with a little more effort I could have become really fluent.

If you have an opportunity to travel to other countries, I urge you to take advantage of it. Learning about other cultures by living in them can be an important part of your education. My time in Panama and Puerto Rico opened my eyes to new cultures and points of view. I also spent an academic year in Rome, Italy, during my sophomore year in college. This experience provided me with a real awakening to classical music, something I've enjoyed for the rest of my life.

Don't be afraid to challenge yourself by taking courses that you know will be difficult. In the long run, whether you make an A, B, or C in a course, especially in high school, will not make that much difference. The important thing is that you learn something—even if that something is learning about yourself.

Don't give short shrift to your religious education. We can't develop a deep faith if we don't know our faith deeply. The only way to know our faith deeply is through study. Unfortunately, many people walk away from the Catholic Faith because they don't really know what they are walking away from. Our faith is very defensible. But we can't defend it or explain it if we don't understand it ourselves. Consider the extent of your knowledge of the Faith when you were an eighth grader. It was pretty basic. Right? If we don't continue to study our faith as we mature and become more sophisticated, we'll find ourselves processing our eighth-grade understanding of the Faith with a much more developed and sophisticated intellect. This is bound to lead to a disconnect. If we want to continue to grow in the Faith, we need to continue to study it. Of course, this does not necessarily mean taking formal courses. I suggest you ask someone you trust, like a good priest, to suggest good books on the Faith to read. These may include doctrinal or other spiritual reading.

On a practical note, I strongly urge you not to take on too much student debt to finance your college education. There are so many stories of college graduates who have to live with their parents and married couples who feel they need to postpone having children due to the mountain of debt they accumulated in college. There are many ways to skin that college financing cat. Be creative! You don't have to finish in four years. You don't have to go to an expensive private school unless they provide plenty of financial aid (grants, not loans). Think this through carefully and avoid being saddled with a ton of school debt.

Finally, if you use your time well, you can pursue your interests in sports and other hobbies and still have the time for outside reading of all sorts. This will make you a more interesting person and open a fascinating world to you.

Affectionately,
Grandpa

Fifteen | Hardships

My Dear Grandchildren,

As you know, hardships are part of life. We all must face them sooner or later. Sometimes they are minor and sometimes they can be severe. You have probably faced some hardships already in your life. Some of the minor hardships you may face include things that are more akin to disappointments. Big disappointments can be very hard to take. They may include such things as failing to make a sports team at school or not getting accepted for admission to the school you really wanted to attend. Another hardship could be a friend who lets you down or a friend who rejects you for some reason. It can be tough if you're shunned by people with whom you'd like to be friends. That can really hurt. These kinds of hardships are real, but over time we tend to get over them and move on with life.

Some hardships are much more serious. For example, parents divorcing, serious illness or death in the family, or a parent's loss of a job for an extended period of time can turn our lives upside down.

When we experience hardships, we tend to feel sorry for ourselves and think that somehow life is not fair. And, of course, life isn't fair. We shouldn't expect it to be. However, I believe things happen for a reason. And our hardships can provide us with an opportunity for growth. We should see these difficulties as the cross that Christ has asked us to bear. They can have redemptive value if we identify our cross with that of our Lord. Our hardships also give others the opportunity to help us. People need to give of themselves. Let them help you. Allow them to be your Simon of Cyrene.

The greatest hardship I experienced was when your grandmother had to have several abdominal surgeries over a period of about five years. She was in and out of the hospital many times. She nearly died on one occasion. This all took place while we had a number of young children to care for. It was beyond stressful. I remember how many of our neighbors, family, and friends organized to provide us with meals during this time. It's a good thing we liked lasagna, because I think every other dinner was some type of lasagna. They also volunteered to watch the kids while I visited Grandma in the hospital. We finally got through this rough patch and Grandma has been quite healthy now for many years. Prayer and the support of our family and friends got us through this difficult time.

Difficulties within the family can spur the family members on to band together to address the problems they face. They can lead to greater family unity. We all know of situations where just the opposite occurs. The difficulties tear a family apart. That's tragic. However, it shouldn't be that way. If we put our trust in God and focus on the others, we can get through any crisis. We all know people who have been able to weather such storms—the death of a child, unemployment, a severe illness. And they do it with cheerfulness and hope. They inspire us.

We all know people who seem to have it all—money, talent, good looks. This, of course, confirms our belief that life isn't fair. But we are just looking at them from the outside. Everyone has problems. These people who seem to have it all have problems too—frequently very big problems. We read about them all the time in the news. Keep in mind that being blessed with wealth and talent comes with a burden. We will all be held accountable for how we use our gifts and talents throughout our lifetime.

Dealing gracefully with our hardships requires a good amount of maturity. That may be more than one can reasonably expect from you at your age. If you are having trouble dealing with the problems you are facing, talk to a trusted friend. The first ones to turn to should be your parents. If for some reason you can't talk to your parents, confide in an adult whom you respect and trust, such as a priest or teacher. The important thing is that you get good, solid advice and counsel, from someone with whom you can share your problems in confidence.

It may be that our Lord allows us to have to deal with hardships so we'll rely on him more. We need to place our problems and difficulties in his hands, while we do everything humanly possible to find solutions to our difficulties. As St. James said, prayer is a powerful antidote to suffering (Jas 5:13). Ask our Lord to help you through your difficulty. You can also ask him to solve the problem you are facing, understanding that his will may be quite different from yours. Try to unite your will to God's. Remember Jesus' prayer in the Garden of Gethsemane when he asked the Father to remove his cup of suffering. But he quickly accepted his Father's will over his own (see Lk 22:42). Jesus has both a human will and a divine will. His human will was horrified by the prospect of the passion and death that he knew he would have to endure. But he united his human will to the divine and went on to redeem us on the cross. When we accept God's will over our own, we too become co-redeemers.

I know this is a lot to take in. And I know dealing with hardships and disappointments is not easy. But if you try to look at your life with a supernatural perspective, place your trust in God, and accept the support of those who care for you, you will emerge from any storm stronger, wiser, and a bit holier.

Affectionately,
Grandpa

Sixteen | Conversion

My Dear Grandchildren,

A religious conversion is not a one-time event. Our first conversion occurs when we make the Catholic Faith our own. This first conversion may not be as dramatic as St. Paul's. We may not be knocked off our horse and blinded by a bright light. In fact, it's more likely to be gradual. When we were little kids, our parents brought us to Mass every Sunday and confession once a month or maybe more often. They taught us our prayers and made sure we learned the doctrine or truths of the Faith in school or at our parish religious education program. They likely supplemented all this with regular discussions about the Catholic Faith and moral issues. As you grew older and more independent, you had to make the Faith your own. This entailed a somewhat subtle form of conversion. Before, it was your parents' faith and you were coming along for the ride. Now you embrace it as your faith.

Some initial conversions are less subtle. Many young people walk away from the Faith in their teens or during their college years. It may be an act of rebellion to some extent or just laziness. In many cases, they were poorly catechized. They were simply not taught the truths of the Faith in a meaningful or convincing manner. Whatever the reason, they stopped practicing the Faith and put God at a distance. For many of these people, a conversion occurred through reading or a good friend or an event in their lives. I fell into this category. It was the prospect of getting married and having children that caused me to snap out of it and take my faith seriously. I certainly wouldn't recommend the path I took to anyone. The preferred road to conversion is the more subtle version described above.

In the long run, however, the most important thing is that the conversion occurs.

Our life will consist of a series of conversions as we struggle to overcome our weaknesses and defects and acquire the virtues. It can be helpful to view our spiritual life as a war with many skirmishes and battles. The spiritual life has been characterized as an inclined plane. We grow in holiness as we progress up the inclined plane. Every step we take forward entails a small conversion. We are generally not stationary on that inclined plane. We either move forward or we slide back, losing ground. So we need to struggle to progress, one step at a time.

Our conversions may involve taking on a defect or vice head on, like pornography or other sins of sensuality, and taking concrete steps to root them out of our lives. It may take the form of recognizing our selfishness and making a resolution to focus on the needs of others.

We can't expect to grow closer to God without a plan of life, a concrete plan that will help us in our struggle to grow in holiness. Our plan of life ought to be demanding, but not all at once. Remember, it's an inclined plane, not an F-16 fighter jet ejector seat. It would be wise and prudent for you to get a spiritual advisor, usually a priest who can help you as you progress on your spiritual journey. Remember, a commitment to seek holiness in your life does not necessarily mean that you are on the path to the priesthood or religious life. Holiness is for everyone, including married people. But you should continue to listen to God's promptings so you'll know the vocation to which you are being called.

Taking that next step in your plan of life may involve a significant conversion, because it requires a leap in generosity. For example, making the commitment to attend daily Mass or praying the Rosary each day would be a significant step. Maybe you haven't been consistent in spending time with our Lord in mental prayer every day. How much time should you commit to? You might start with fifteen minutes a day. Your spiritual advisor can help you with that. But regularly conversing with our Lord is necessary if we truly desire to foster a friendship with him. It's a big step, a life-changing step requiring a true conversion of heart.

Keep in mind that you will not realize your need for conversion unless you strive to know yourself well. You'll grow in self-knowledge with prayer and a deep examination of conscience each day. Also, take advantage of an annual retreat and regular days of recollection. These will help you immensely in assessing whether you need a course correction.

We all need regular conversions in our lives, if nothing else to recommit ourselves to the path we are called to follow. The devil will offer us many appealing alternatives. (Yes, there is a devil and he would love it if you would not believe that.) So, keep up the struggle—a joyful struggle!

Affectionately,
Grandpa

Conclusion

This little book has covered a lot of ground. It challenges young people to be the best they can be, to be all that God intends them to be. Some of what I've shared with you is just my opinion. However, I think it is all good advice that can lead our grandchildren closer to God, help them to be better friends, better husbands or wives, and better citizens. You can adapt these ideas to your own situation, reflecting your own experience. The bottom line is that we do what we can to help our grandchildren pursue a life that flourishes. We can help them become great lovers, which means to help them to know how to give of themselves. Loving is sacrificial. We will have lived a successful life if we love a lot—love God, our family, our friends, and our neighbors. We will all become better lovers as we grow in the virtues and overcome our defects and weaknesses. Of course, we know that life is a struggle. But we can help our grandkids acquire a sporting spirit, as they make progress little by little.